MW01167530

- BOOK ONE -

All That Is

Seth Returns Publishing
Lake County California

Copyright © 2010 by Mark Allen Frost

Published by Seth Returns Publishing
Lake County California

Editorial: Mark Allen Frost
Cover Art, Design, Typography & Layout: Mark Frost

Library of Congress Control Number: 2010901053

ISBN: 978-0-9740586-9-6

This book is dedicated with love and gratitude to The Warrior. Thanks for everything Dad.

Many thanks to Walter Zweifel, Klaus Shulte and Boris N. Krivoruk for their generous contributions to this project.

CONTENTS

ACT ONE

Who Is In Charge?
Here In this Moment
When You Walk Across the Room
You Are a Part of Everything
Everything Is a Part of You
In Cooperation with Birds
The "Wake" of Spirit
Everything Means Something
Spontaneous Expression of All Forms
Tuning Your Consciousness
Awakening
Intellectualization
Denial
Creating Lack
The Visionary State
Experimenting with the Divine
Embody the Forces of Nature
Experiment: Talking to Storms

ALL THAT IS

ACT TWO

ACT THREE

CONTENTS

With Whose Eyes?
Negative Bleedthroughs
The 2012 Phenomenon
Technique: Sensing the Positive Manifestation
The Epiphany
Past Life Payback
Suggestions Clarifications
The Spiritual Hierarchy
Personalizing the Divine Energies
God
The Graphic Representation
Religious Authority
Inflated Ego/intellect
Experiment: Polarizing the Inflated Ego/
intellect

INTRODUCTION BY MARK

Welcome to the new Seth book. This one is based on what Seth calls his "little essays." You could also call them extended talking points, inspired comments, or even jumping-off places for further discussion. On the surface it appears that he is making simple statements that the reader must take on faith. But if you work with this material I think you will begin to understand the deeper meaning.

Here again, Seth is keeping his promise to explore the spiritual aspects of reality. As he teaches me how to appreciate the spiritual within my own personal reality, he is also demonstrating the importance of Spirit for the reader. That's his plan.

The experiments are presented as in past books, with a suggested hypothesis and a request to the researcher to document their Findings from the investigation. I am aware this may be an affront to some of our scientists. That's OK. I think Seth is trying to make a point here about the value of this type of research.

You can open the book anywhere and begin reading. It works because Seth put it together in a nonlinear fashion, perhaps reflecting the true nature of time. As he told me humorously in the second session when I asked him how he experiences time: "Time? Right! There IS no time."

Seth chose the smaller format so that readers could take books "into the Field." He spoke of the reader putting the book in their pocket and heading out to do research.

Key concepts are again capitalized. We have no Index but we do offer you pull quotes, descriptive heads, and a Table of Contents that lists the titles of all Seth's essays.

... denotes a pause in Seth's dictation.

Enjoy.

INTRODUCTION BY SETH

Seth, do you want to outline the All That Is project?

Yes Mark. Very simply now, as you have just perceived... a beginning, a middle, and an end; three acts, as it were. The first act notes the co-creation of realities in the moment by everything. Mark, you will be the visionary here as I inspire you with Holographic Inserts. It is a matter of opening up to your greater awareness and then documenting the moment-to-moment experiencing of this VISION. I would suggest you create Sanctuary before these voyages. Place yourself in a relaxed, focused state free from distractions for specific amounts of time. You may begin after these preparations by asking for inspiration.

Act two: your Lessons impinge upon your Reality Creation strategies and serve to spin you off onto alternate paths of development. You are born in Love, but you learn your Lessons through encountering the Negative Emotions.

And Act three: conscious co-creation entails the intentional learning of Lessons. The Lessons of physical existence are not denied nor are they intellectualized. This is also what you call Enlightenment or Soul Evolution.

This will be a Seth book. I do not envision another *The God of Jane* type volume. We shall attempt to engage the reader in an understanding and appreciation of their divine heritage. No Q and A. We shall create a mood of sacred understanding. The book will begin at the beginning and end at the current Moment Point that the reader is reading The End.

YOU ARE AWAKENING NOW

In this conversation we are having within these pages, it will seem as though I Seth am the one who is doing all the talking. However, listen carefully to the inner voice of yours, the intuitive voice, and you may hear the give-and-take of divine information that occurs on the level of the Soul Self. Because I am speaking to you from within your own consciousness, you could say that these messages are a loving gift from yourself, as we are all of us a part of the great cosmic center of all realities.

To others observing you as you read this little book, it may appear that you are quite engrossed in the subject matter, with furrowed brow and mouth agape. Indeed, I suggest you surrender yourself to these messages. Allow your inner being to inquire of this communication stream the Lessons to be learned for you in your current lifetime. The answers will come to you mentally, as you continue to read, or perhaps when you have put down the book and are resting comfortably. We call these personalized messages Holographic Inserts. They are teaching aids created to further your understanding in the moment and to facilitate your awakening.

"What am I awakening to?" you might ask. You are awakening to yourself - your greater self. This greater self of which you are a part, and upon which you are based, is what we are calling All That Is in this manuscript.

PREFACE

We have divided the book into three sections and have created essays and examples that fall generally under the three separate headings. However, Dear Reader, we are always speaking of the same subject here in my new books. The subject is always Reality Creation - manifestation - and the goal is always the same: to attempt to not persuade, as much as to <u>validate</u> for the reader.

We are not in these books out to "change your mind," nor are we trying to offend you with our unconventional theories. We are quite honestly reminding you of something you already know. The inherent contradiction in this statement holds the key to your understanding, if you wish to understand.

Then the other side of this issue - of purpose, of mission, you might also say - is this: we write these new books for a particular readership. Yes, we are reminding you of something you already know, something you have learned throughout your many lives. However, we are certain that you are of this group of humans that is trying to remember. You are most probably on a quest for understanding. That is why you are drawn to these new books. That is why you find the material intriguing. It reminds you of something.

If you have trouble understanding the concepts herein, consult the glossary at the back of the manuscript. Also, please be advised that there is a subtext here that you may tune-in on with your intuitive senses. There is more to the printed word, as usual. There is as much here, indeed, as you could possibly need for your explorations of consciousness. Dig deep, therefore, and take what you feel speaks to you personally. It may be that I have presented that piece expressly for you, to assist you in your awakening.

ACT ONE

(Awakening)

The first act notes the co-creation of realities in the moment by everything. Mark, you will be the visionary here as I inspire you with Holographic Inserts.

AWAKENING

You have made the weather to suit your own needs and likes…

Who Is In Charge?

Beauty creates itself within the mind of the beholder <u>first</u>. All of the streams of information that you would care to notice, including the rich source that flows into your personal field of reality, first bubble up to the surface of <u>your</u> consciousness. Then they are displayed by you, for you to observe.

To marvel at the beauty, then, of a tree, or a beautiful animal such as a horse, is <u>self</u>-complimentary. If you are having sunny weather and that is your favorite style of weather, then congratulate yourself; you have made the weather to suit your own needs and likes.

You create the weather as surely as you create everything within your personal world. Particularly within your immediate vicinity, your reality does spring into being in unison with the creative content of your mind.

Now with this description questions of control may come to mind. Who is in charge? Who is the ultimate creator, the God of your world? These are questions best answered by the reader.

The thought-created masterpiece…

Here in This Moment

Here in this moment rests your world, the Universe, the entirety of being. Thoughts both pleasant and mild, as well as unpleasant and insistent, paint the landscape with their content. Your thoughts, the thoughts of your neighbors, friends and family, the thoughts of tree, of spider, of glass, of stone, mingle in the alchemy of creation. The living landscape that is the thought-created masterpiece of the human intelligence, stands within and is influenced by the greater elemental works created and sustained by the tree, the glass, the stone, the spider. All is related in the cooperative venture of world realized.

The stone dislodged, the glass cracked, the spider forced to spin a different web through the interference of wind or human, comprehensively alters the momentary creation of world. The novel thought considered by the solitary human, alters to the atomic level, the entire creation of world. The implications of inter-connectedness are such that the human consciousness can be both humbled and elevated simultaneously. Ecstasy.

AWAKENING

*So it is not a matter of "bringing" your body
across the room…*

When You Walk Across the Room

Dear Reader, when you walk across the room, you are with each movement forward, re-creating your physical body according to your essential identity out of the Consciousness Units that exist as air in front of you; space, you see. It is not a matter of "bringing" your body across the room; it is more a case of re-creating your body in its totality within this field - within this medium, if you prefer - of holographic units of awarized energy: the Consciousness Units.

Step-by-step, then, your sacred identity - this Soul Self - assembles the physical body of you-the-reader from the CUs "in front of it." The CUs - identified as atoms, or molecules, or CUs of air - are transformed into CUs of blood, flesh, and bone.

Now… in the same precise fashion, the birds as they swoop down to feed, are creating from the CUs of air before them, their bird bodies.

But what of the tree, the mountain, you might ask? As the tree sways in the wind, it re-creates itself out of the CUs of earth and air surrounding it. As the mountain endures the weathering forces of rain and wind, it retains its mountain identity and re-creates itself with minute or catastrophic alterations, according to this weathering over time.

He is composed of CUs of the same generic type...

You Are a Part of Everything

You are a part of everything. We continue to affirm this fact for you-the-reader, not to give you an elevated sense of your own worth, but to simply state for you the facts of your existence.

What is reality? What is the truth of the matter? These are philosophical questions that drive the enquiring mind. (humorously) Here we are making our case that you are both the creator and the experiencer of your reality.

An illustration is in order... My colleague Mark has taken to riding the bus rather than driving his own vehicle. He has found that it frees him up to do writing and to commune with other humans; something he both desires and needs, as in the basic <u>human</u> needs. As he was, moments ago as we write this, observing two large pine trees that stand at the entrance to the casino at which he was waiting for the bus, a huge beautiful hawk burst out of one tree, and effortlessly, silently, flew off to the surrounding countryside.

He did indeed marvel at this exhibition of beautiful Mother Nature, and he asked himself, as he often does now, "What does that mean?" It occurred to him that there was meaning in this event on many levels. However, there were two primary meanings or Lessons in this evocative scene:

First: He was reminded that he is a part of everything and everything is a part of him, for he briefly projected his consciousness into that of the hawk's, and accompanied the animal for a short distance. He was able to do this for he is composed of CUs of the same generic type that the hawk is composed. So this was an endorsement from Spirit - All That Is - to him, of his current trajectory of Soul Evolution.

Second: He had a deja vu experience. He seemed to remember a conversation with a local Native American, in which the subject of the sacred hawk that lives in the twin pines of the Twin Pines Casino arose. It seemed to Mark at the time that the fellow was quite urgent in his telling this tale of the hawk. Perhaps, thought Mark, the fellow was setting the stage for his "future" experiencing of this hawk, the guardian of the Twin Pines area. It did seem to Mark that the experience was perceived "out-of-time," in a dream-like encounter with the natural world.

The whole is found within the part...

Everything Is a Part of You

Your Universe is experienced by you, <u>through</u> you; through the physical body, the physical senses; and so you feel as though you are "taking in" your experience <u>through</u> your perceptions, from the outside in. Yet you know by now that it is just the opposite, in truth. The Universe, All That Is, the entire creation of physical reality exists <u>within you</u> in the collaborative moment. In each moment you project your personalized "take" on the state of the Universe outward into the Third Dimension. So you could truly say that everything that exists on the Earth at any one time, first exists within your consciousness "before" it is projected out onto your world.

You have limited perception in the Third Dimension, however, and you do not see everything within your cozy little Personal Reality. Depending on your Issues or Lessons, you may see very little at all in this personalized world view. Yet the potential is there to use your Inner Senses to discover within your world, the answers to any questions you may have on any subject whatsoever.

The whole is found within the part. The world is found within the individual. You are a part of everything and everything is a part of you.

This synchronicity of creation…

In Cooperation With Birds

Now my friend Mark here is just this moment observing the behavior of birds feeding from his sunflower seeds that he replenishes each morning. In a quite delightful fashion, the creatures swoop in to take what they need and fly out to eat their meal. There is great cooperation here, even when the larger jays squawk in defense of "their" food source. Even the jay, then, allows the smaller birds to take food.

As Mark observed this activity, it occurred to him that there was a direct correlation, somehow, between the precise activities of the birds and his own mental activity. He sensed that the cooperative effort included his personal thoughts and images.

Let me elaborate... your Personal Reality Field IS a cooperative effort or presentation involving the manifestation energies and agendas of each and every CU composing each and every bird, rock, tree, or human existing within this field of awareness. This synchronicity of creation, you see, is evident down to the last detail.

The Loving creative thrust of All That Is...

The "Wake" of Spirit

This wind that you observe by its activity, its effects - as in moving the leaves and limbs of a great tree, for example - is an emotional response. Let me explain: You already know that everything in your world is conscious, as All That Is - of which you and your Personal Reality Field are composed - presents itself. All That Is - evolutionary consciousness - may be considered, then, in its totality as a sensing, emoting being. Each CU is also an emotional, sensing being unto itself.

We could compare the emotional life of, let us say, a bird, to that of a rock, or any other Reality Construct within your system, including the emoting human. If we were to do so we would find that EVERYTHING experiences emotion, the same basic emotion, in quite similar ways. This foundational emotion expressed by all within your world, we could call the Loving creative <u>thrust</u> of All That Is.

Again, we are presenting this material in fairly mechanical terms. I repeat: You are not a machine! Yet this metaphor of the student "pushing" the Reality Construct from the potential into the actual with their Intent, may once again assist us in our explanations.

Everything is composed of consciousness and everything is a reality creator. Each Reality Construct expresses itself in the medium of divine energy some of you call God - the Spirit. The Thrust is Love with a capital L. The energy for creation is Love.

The wind has been called "the breath of God." You could also call it the "wake" of Spirit, as in the turbulence created by a vessel or airplane. The wind is the reciprocal emotional expression of the natural world. It is a response to the Loving creation of realities out of Consciousness Units.

Now this Love with a capital L is not evident until the moment of creation. When that moment occurs and All That Is expresses itself as whatever varied construct, Love becomes evident. You can see it.

You are building this current pleasant moment…

Everything Means Something

Everything means something. Each perception may be followed back to its source within your creative consciousness. When you are experiencing a pleasant moment in your personal reality, for example, if you were to follow back this episode to its source, you might observe how every atom that composes your perceptual field - including the reality constructs you call trees, animals, humans, newspapers - is fabricated from pleasant feelings, positive emotions, and images from your past, current, and dare I say, "future" consciousness. You are building this current pleasant moment upon a foundation of "remembered" positive-experiencing, to the degree that your personal consciousness - including your belief system, your memories, your cosmology - imbues all that you perceive with pleasantness.

Now you could just as easily in the next moment of creation turn the tables here, and imbue your Personal Reality Field with negative emotion and negative imagery using denial and intellectualization. It is up to you. You decide - for the most part unconsciously - which way to go with the creation of your world.

Given this truth, do you now understand how peace, abundance-for-all, and any other wholesome concept exists as a potential CHOICE for individuals and groups? Your individual and collective realities <u>result</u> from the individual and collective choices of humans to create and perceive in the positive, in the negative, or in the vast area in between.

You are ONE with nature…

The Spontaneous Expression of All Forms

This is our concept for discussion at this time. Now there exists a barrier to understanding for some of you that prevents your <u>intellect</u> from accepting the fantastic premise that you cooperate with All That Is in the <u>literal</u> creation of your physical world. This barrier is one of the last to fall as you approach your awakening. Let me set the stage, if I may…

You are in nature, in a forest, writing in your journal, and you are approached by a deer. You are motionless and quiet as the deer comes closer and closer to you, so close in fact that you could reach out and touch it. As you quietly contemplate this miracle of nature, a pair of quail walk onto the scene. They too are oblivious of you as they stroll past, again, within arm's reach.

Then, as if to further impress you, Dear Reader, the birds in the trees fly quickly past you to perch on nearby branches and to feed directly next to you. You are <u>still</u> here. You are quiet. You are ONE with nature. This is the perfect state for experiencing the Divine. The ego/intellect is off to the side, out of the way of your perception, as the Soul Self observes/creates your Personal Reality.

Ah, but then you make an abrupt motion with your hand to write down what you are experiencing. The ego/intellect has taken charge. The animals disperse in alarm. The fragile moment of appreciation has passed.

Now moments later the animals have again taken their places within nature, in that timeless moment <u>beyond</u> ego, <u>beyond</u> the intellect, <u>beyond</u> the rational mind. However, as you take your notes in your journal you are merely a reporter commenting on the preceding events. Your ego/intellect has taken you <u>out</u> of the moment. Whereas the "dumb" animals, as you call them, for they lack your rationality, continue their precisely focused existences in the moment - the divine moment of creation.

The moment of perception gains a fullness,
an energized complexity...

Tuning Your Consciousness

An awakening of your personal consciousness to All That Is is possible for you in any chosen moment in your waking reality. It becomes a matter of <u>intentionally</u> perceiving your world through the auspices, you might say, of the Divine. If you have meditated, if you have prayed, if you have experimented with your conscious Intent, you have already used your perceptions in this divine way I am describing.

Have you noticed while engaged in these common practices, that the moment of perception gains a fullness, an energized complexity? If you have noticed this pleasant "pressing in" of the energies upon your consciousness, you may also be adept at "tuning" this state to meet your requirements. The depth of your meditation may be increased or decreased, in other words. The profoundness of your trance may be increased or decreased, simply by using your Intent.

We refer to these empowered moments of Intent as Moment Points. They are essentially gateways to a broader perception of your world and your place in it. You are a researcher of your experience in your waking reality. Each moment holds the potential for revealing to you the answers to any questions you might have. It is up to <u>you</u> to focus on the business at hand - your awakening - and delve deeply within the moment. Briefly: it is your Moment Point if you say it is. Own your current moment, therefore, and awaken to your greater reality.

The negative emotions are the creators of states of consciousness and thus personal realities...

Awakening

To simplify for you this awakening experience, we have described it as a matter of transforming the negative emotions into their opposites. We will now add to this with an example. Now the negative emotions are the creators of states of consciousness and thus personal realities. These emotions run the course from fairly harmless, such as mild irritation, shall we say, to murderous anger at the other pole of this comparison.

We are speaking of anger here. However, with the emotion of fear, we could also place it on a scale, perhaps beginning with a subtle anxiety in the financial realms, as the negative media continually remind you of the treacherous state of the world through your television or radio. So you are a wee bit anxious on this side of our theoretical pole, but if you were to exist on the opposite end here, you would be experiencing aghast dread and fear for your existence, possibly. You may fill in the "reasons" for this ruinous state of affairs.

Let us then examine where your Intention or Will resides within this matrix of emotional experiencing. We have said before that if you are experiencing extreme anger or fear in any particular moment, you are no longer "in control" of your consciousness. You have relinquished control of your Reality Creation powers to the Negative Emotions. You are assisting in the re-creation, moment-to-moment, of these emotions through this shirking of responsibility.

As you, Dear Reader, lay the blame for your negative states of consciousness on the doorstep of your neighbor, friends, family, or colleagues, not only do you dis-empower yourself, but you help to empower the negative spheres of influence, what we have called the Negative Entities in these pages.

Now we have a sense of humor about these naysayers,
for we know the truth here...

Intellectualization

If I may, I would enjoy providing for you an example of intellectualization as it pertains to a group we refer to as the naysayers. Members of this group of humans may be found within any collective, large or small. Within what we are calling the Seth community broadly speaking, these humans often are the most vocal in their refusals to accept my new messages.

Now we have a sense of humor about these naysayers, for we know the truth here. And there is irony, in that, those who consider themselves "experts" on my writings, are at times the most vociferous in their denials of my return. Those who have not heard of my works, on the other hand, are much more likely to embrace my new messages with an open mind and heart. Perhaps they are not looking to authorities to tell them what to believe.

And thus it appears that it is this calcified knowledge of the authority that prevents the clear perception of what is in front of them. However, we could also be speaking about any other authority that refutes what you might call "anecdotal" information from the common citizen.

What is at fault here is a form of circular logic, and the naysayer often speaks from within this twisted knot of intellectualization and denial to make their case and to present "the historical facts." In essence they are saying, "My personal perceptions are the only reality here. What I believe and what the other authorities believe is what everyone must believe."

The intellect proves the beliefs of the authority. Stability in the Reality Creation agenda of the individual is achieved in this way. If they feel as though they have proved their case adequately, there is then no need to expand the belief system to include the new data. The calcification of knowledge continues. The avoidance of Lessons is perfected.

Perhaps you are somewhat cynical of these ideas, yet you are looking for "something to believe in..."

Denial

How does this intellectualization and denial fit in with our discussion of All That Is? In all of your existence, Dear Reader, in each of your experienced moments in physical reality, there is the potential for awakening to the spiritual realm, the Divine, All That Is. We state this as fact even though we know that you may not consider yourself on a spiritual path. Perhaps you are reading this volume out of curiosity only. Perhaps you are somewhat cynical of these ideas, yet you are looking for "something to believe in." Here is where our concept of denial enters the picture.

Let us assume that you are the somewhat "cynical scientist." You are perhaps of an atheistic bent or agnostic, and you are looking for "something," something in the spiritual realm. You have led a life free of spirituality, either by choice or chance, and you have reached a stage in your life, perhaps after a brush with death yourself, or after the death of a loved-one, when you are contemplating the validity of the spiritual life.

In the nomenclature of our system, we would say that "the denial is lifting for you." You are no longer denying the spiritual within your existence. As you release your

nomemclature

perceptions from the task of denying the obvious spiritual basis of reality, you immediately begin to find evidence for Spirit. Indeed, you may begin to see the spiritual in each moment of your life.

If this is the case, you may identify yourself as one of the awakening ones of your timeframe. Millions of you are seeking out the spiritual within your lives. You are coming out of your denial and finding All That Is within your personal realities.

You limit yourself if you believe
you have limitations...

Creating Lack

You limit yourself if you believe you have limitations. In truth, there are no limits to what you may create. You may see this for yourself by observing what surrounds you in your personal reality. A true appreciation of your surroundings would convince you, that, as the creator of your world, you have great talents and energies at your disposal.

Of course it is also true that there may be for you the <u>absence</u> of what you truly desire within your self-created world. We call this Lack in the books. If you are seeing the element of Lack in your reality, can you also see the founding beliefs of that Lack?

Your beliefs create your reality. If you are seeing the absence of what you desire in front of you, you may trace that back to your own creative consciousness. It is there that you may receive an intuition of what is holding you back from creating abundance. The beliefs that you are using as a blueprint for the creation of your reality may be self-limiting. Look for where you limit yourself. Move beyond those self-imposed limitations and see the infinite creativity that is your birthright.

We are speaking of the magic ancestors here…

The Visionary State

In the new manuscripts I often bow to the superior wisdom of your human ancestors, the native peoples of your continents, the aboriginals who came before, the First People. Much was lost when the developing human moved beyond the simplicity of existence that denoted tribal living.

Yet make no mistake here, I am not advocating a "noble savage" perspective. I am merely noting that your individual, pioneer mentality was won at great cost, as in the effects of splintering the collective gestalt that was the nurturing mental environment of your ancestors.

We are speaking of the magic ancestors here, and we are speaking of the time when ALL of you appreciated the magical approach. You were all visionaries then, and you each and every one were capable of wonder-workings of various types. Yet even now as you observe yourself in the modern era, perhaps detached from a collective of any meaning, you are still quite capable of attaining the visionary state of your ancestors through some thoughtful, focused experimentation.

Now the power of nature is the power of your system of reality. Your Earth and Sky were formed by the powers of nature, and in the words of your visionaries, the "miracle of creation" was a participatory event. Much in the way that the modern sports enthusiast participates in sporting events by watching and becoming emotionally involved, the magic ancestors participated in the give-and-take of the natural energies as they observed Mother Nature creating the Earth and Sky. We have called this involvement in various gestalts of consciousness "embodiment." This is our modern term for participatory engagement with the Divine, or co-creation as some of you call it.

> *Make the preparations for physical*
> *and emotional Sanctuary…*

Experimenting with the Divine

You may co-create the visionary experience anywhere you happen to be at the moment. It does not necessarily require you to be in nature, but it does seem to be one of the only times that the modern human may take some time out to relax and go within.

Let us say, for the sake of experimenting, that you are in your workplace relaxing by yourself, or you are in a public place being observed by others around you, yet you are eager to make contact with the Divine and achieve some sort of visionary perception. You may do so with these cautions in mind: You will be vulnerable in the visionary state. Make the preparations for physical and emotional Sanctuary, therefore, before you begin.

See the Ritual of Sanctuary at the end of the manuscript for instructions on how to achieve Sanctuary.

You may also create the suggestion within your consciousness that you will be available for spontaneous disengagement from the visionary state if you NEED to be, as in an emergency situation that may arise. Also, if you find that your protected state is lessening due to circumstances mental or physical, and you are allowing yourself to become anxious, fearful etc., take your cue from the suggestion that you will be able to easily exit the visionary state of consciousness and attain fully alert and conscious use of your faculties.

Now suppose it is raining and storming outside, and you may see the effects through the window. You may hear the thunder and see the rain and the lightning. You may see the effects of the wind as it blows the leaves down the street. What are you observing, in fact? It is our understanding that you are witnessing the cathartic effects of the collective emotional energies of the consensus reality in which you live.

This is a very powerful and necessary demonstration of consciousness creation of the collective, here. Yet many are frightened by the display of nature, some to the degree that they will stay indoors with the shades closed, trembling in fear of the potentially destructive power wielded by Mother Nature. But let us take advantage of these energies with a simple experiment.

Participating in the storm by lending your subconscious emotional energies...

Embody the Forces of Nature

In the following experiment let us assume the opposite perspective. We are not frightened, we are courageously engaging the storm. Now, just as you, Dear Reader, as an emoting human being, on occasion are subject to tears of distress and joy, so too is the emoting being your Mother Earth subject to the powerful displays of emotional energy called rainstorms. The correlations are available "to the nth degree," as we say.

Consider the convulsive grieving and sobbing of the human after the loss of a loved one. Compare this momentous emotion-charged activity with a rainstorm. It is the same process in principle. The rainstorm is the collective manifestation of the thought and emotion-charged energies of thousands and hundreds of thousands of humans.

Now, you know that you create the weather with your thoughts and emotions. It may be an acceptable belief to you at this point. Can you then enlarge and deepen this belief to include a participatory element here, an exchange between you-the-reader - the Scientist of Consciousness - and the storm? Yes, you are already participating in the storm by lending your subconscious emotional energies to the manifestation. Your repressed memories of grief, losses of various types, and frustration, enter into the creation of the storm.

There are several ways to make this participation conscious if you wish to gain the full healing potential of the dramatic storm event. If it is appropriate for you at this time, as you sit at your desk at work or otherwise out in the public arena, consider YOUR PART in the dramatic presentation of Mother Nature that you call "rainstorm." Using your intent, you will gently probe the psychic climate initiated by the storm, and see your contribution. You will observe this in your personalized fashion, as you do in all of our experimentation that we do together. But let me suggest that you proceed in this way:

Experiment - Talking to Storms
Hypothesis: you can reclaim and process your cast-off emotional contribution to the storm

Perform Your Ritual of Sanctuary

Consider these talking points for talking to storms.

♦ You are connected to Mother Nature and the elements directly.

♦ You have a hand in the literal creation of storm activities.

♦ This contribution is largely anonymous, as well as unconscious.

♦ You may "remember" your subconscious contribution by considering what "comes up" for you during this storm.

♦ Are your Issues triggered by the storm?

♦ Are you attempting to keep something down, something buried beneath the facade of your public persona?

♦ Would it be appropriate to write down what you are feeling now in this moment?

♦ If so, write down what you are experiencing that you feel may be related to the storm.

I do realize that it would most likely be <u>in</u>-appropriate for you to engage in a cathartic moment of grief-full sobbing. Yet you may certainly make an appointment with yourself to do just that at another time, possibly when you are alone or with a trusted friend.

Do not be surprised when your cathartic acceptance of the repressed negative material gives way to celebratory emotions of joy, forgiveness, compassion, ecstasy. As the negative aspects of repressed emotion are realized, there is often a great flood of emotion that is released. This creative energy may be used to advantage, particularly in your attempts to experience the communication stream of All That Is or in any other creative pursuits.

Findings: Please document your Findings

_____
_____
_____
_____
_____
_____

ACT TWO

(Lessons)

Your Lessons impinge upon your Reality Creation
strategies and serve to spin you off onto alternate paths
of development. You are born in Love, but you learn
your Lessons through encountering
the Negative Emotions.

LESSONS

You will also sense a growing humility…

You Create Your Own Reality

The thoughts you think, the images you imagine, seek out fulfillment through manifestation in your system and other dimensions. As the mask of your camouflage reality is lifted, you will see this truth of your physical existence. You will notice with increasing frequency how your perceptions seem to support the notion that you create your own reality. It will become commonplace for you to marvel, perhaps, at the immediate manifestation of something you had hoped for, prayed for, or visualized. You will be receiving the proofs you require to change or expand your beliefs.

So now you know. You are the creator of your world, quite literally. Perhaps in these moments of awakening to your true nature, you will also sense a growing humility that parallels the growth of your new powers of perception. With the witnessing of your reality creation powers you may also realize your responsibilities - your responsibilities to your self, your family, and to humanity. Acknowledging your responsibilities to create your world for the highest good, for the good of all, is often accompanied by a growing sense of awe, gratitude, and humility within the personal consciousness.

This is how you define all stimuli that comes to you through your physical senses...

Accepted or Rejected Reality Fields

As you read these words what is taking place within your consciousness? There is only the momentary acceptance or denial of what you are perceiving/creating. Second-to-second you create a cohesive reality that reflects your beliefs. But suppose that you read a sentence that is difficult for you to entertain as fact? In the moment there may be a split second of hesitation as you decide whether to incorporate this statement into your Personal Reality Field. If you accept it, the statement will be submitted as proof that ALL of the statements in this manuscript have validity. Otherwise, YOU would know of the invalid nature of the statement.

You are the authority here, yet you are always attempting to prove to some "higher authority" within your consciousness that you are correct in your assumptions about the trivia within your self-created existence. If the material meets your standards of truth, it is accepted and incorporated into your Reality Creation agendas. If it doesn't meet your criteria for validity according to your beliefs, it is rejected.

Additionally, all corresponding and supporting data connected to the rejected field of information is also rejected. The belief system is kept intact through this process. The ego/intellect is supported and affirmed in its thoughts and behaviors in this way. Accepted or rejected: this is how you define all stimuli that comes to you through your physical senses.

There is spontaneity and there is spontaneity...

Spontaneity and the Moment Point

When you are in your Issues and succumbing to the forces of negativity, you are not consciously co-creating your world; you are being driven by the negative emotions to continue to create negative emotions and the negative realities that ensue when you focus on the negative. It is primarily a subconscious process, as we have said.

In my system, as in some others you might name, the process of change is quite simple; fear is transformed into Courage in the moment, anger into Loving Understanding. This is how we create positive realities.

Now there is spontaneity and there is spontaneity. Do you see how you may spontaneously, "on impulse" as you

31

say, re-create anger in your current moments. Over-and-over you create anger - second-to-second, minute-to-minute, and hour-to-hour - until you have created "spontaneously" a negative state of consciousness for yourself. From my perspective, this is not spontaneity nor is it acting on impulses. This is simply the habitual creation of negative states. It is irresponsible and it is largely counter-productive for the individual.

True spontaneity is not the robotic re-creation of the current emotional state. It is not reaction without direction. In the true spontaneous moment there is a brief pause of reflection that occurs. One responds to the positive, to the positive manifestation, rather than the negative. One responds to the divine emotions, you might say, rather than the baser emotions. The choice is made in this pause of reflection to do the right thing. And you do.

*I am responsible for both the negative
and the positive in my world...*

Intellectualization and Denial

Now, intellectualization and denial are your friends here as you attempt to avoid your Lessons. (humorously) You are all powerful. You have the capacity to experience your world as the Logos, the Creator, All That Is. You could have anything you want, potentially, anything you would wish to create.

However, you are a human experiencing a lifetime of Lessons on your world. You have forgotten - the necessary amnesia - your great powers, and now you see difficulties, Lack, all sorts of negative realities before you. So intellectualization helps you to find reasons for the negative realities you are creating. Denial helps you place the blame elsewhere for your negative states and your negative realities.

But look... an inkling of the truth is beginning to pierce the veil of illusion that is your perceived reality. You are beginning to see the connections between your negative thoughts and the negative outcomes. Slowly you are formulating within your consciousness a new paradigm of understanding. Perhaps it goes something like this: I am responsible for both the negative and the positive in my world. All the reasons, in truth, point to my culpability in all instances of my existence.

Challenge your own beliefs
about your world...

What Do You See In Front Of You?

What do You See In Front Of You? You see All That Is in front of you. Everything in created reality is in front of you for you to see. But you have lenses of perception that prevent you from seeing ALL that is. You must filter All That Is through these lenses – beliefs – so that you are not awestruck, dumbfounded, fascinated to the extreme, every time you look in front of you.

However, if you believe our assertion that great numbers of you are awakening at this time, you may also see what is required for you and your perception of your world. In a sense, you could say that you are being challenged to "look beyond" your limited beliefs of what is out there in front of you. You are being asked to, courageously now, challenge your own beliefs about your world.

So when I suggest that Mark, for example, as he observes his bird friends bathing, drinking water, and eating the seeds, is also experimenting with a perception of the larger view – the macrocosm – I am simply noting what many of you are now experiencing.

Specifically now... as Mark observes the birds, he may also fairly easily observe his Personal Reality Field through a "higher" perspective. This perspective is that of the Soul Self, the Energy Personality, the god within. Both perspectives – the mundane and the exalted – coexist without interference one from the other. In fact, each perspective endorses, and in a sense, "comments" upon the other, in a quest for further understanding, a clearer perspective, Enlightenment. Multitasking we call it. You are quite comfortably maintaining your Personal Reality Field through your ego/intellect perspective, while also achieving stability observing and creating through the Soul Self.

*The ego/intellect is heavily invested
in appearances…*

Resisting and Letting-go

How do you distinguish between these two vastly different perspectives, that of the Soul Self on the one hand, and the ego/intellect on the other? The emotional tone generated is quite different; the opposite, in fact, of the other. It is the difference, as we have stated to our Internet audience, between conscious co-creation and unconscious creation. It is the difference, particularly in matters of Lessons, between resisting in the Moment Point, and letting-go in the Moment Point.

It is obvious, is it not, that <u>when</u> you resist, <u>when</u> you attempt to control, <u>when</u> you attempt to intellectualize, rationalize, think-things-through, you are perceiving through a particular lens of Reality Creation? This we call the ego/intellect.

Conversely, <u>when</u> you let go, <u>when</u> you go-with-the-flow of manifestation, <u>when</u> you take your place within nature within the elemental forces, you are creating through the perspective of the timeless Soul Self. The differences are striking; unmistakable really.

For example: If you are angrily reacting to a conversation you are hearing on your radio or television and you are stomping around the room in a huff, what perspective are you embodying? If you are hiding behind the furniture when the bill collector knocks on the door, what perspective are you embodying?

The ego/intellect is heavily invested in appearances. The ego in particular has distinct preferences for how others should perceive it. There is much of perceived value that must be protected. In this process, whole aspects of the personality and Soul are drawn under, disavowed, and denied. These unpleasant facts of the personality assemble in the creation of the disowned self, what we refer to as the Negative Persona, which we shall discuss at the end of this section.

*This multitasking may produce profound insights
into thoughts and behaviors…*

The Observer Perspective

Do you notice the difference here between conscious and unconscious creation? In my new books we discuss a valuable exercise for the student: Embodying the Observer Perspective. One simply creates a personality aspect or aspect of the personal consciousness that observes objectively the events within the life.

This multitasking may produce profound insights into thoughts and behaviors. You are experiencing and remembering in this perspective BOTH the unconscious creation of realities and the conscious creation of realities. The two merge in the beginning of your studies, as you learn how to distinguish the one from the other. Then as you master the technique, you find that you may easily embody the observer perspective for successive moments, minutes, and even hours. You are making the unconscious conscious in this way.

Put another way... the explorer voyages into and through the unknown reality and Courageously and Lovingly acknowledges ALL that is found within this underground of the personal psyche. A broader perspective is obtained in this exploration.

And another... the conscious is taken into the subconscious ritually. Over time the two perspectives meld one to the other. As awakening occurs the Observer Perspective becomes enriched by both conscious and unconscious material. The synthesis of the two perspectives creates the Enlightened or Visionary consciousness.

It is as though the subconscious is helping you to face the music...

You Are Challenged by the Negative

As a creator of realities you witness your mental and emotional material projected outward into physicality. Because this is, for the most part, a subconscious activity, as we have said, this feedback that is the Personal Reality

37

Field may contain some disagreeable elements as in fear and anger-inspiring events - the Reincarnational Dramas.

This material "slips out" from the subconscious through the censor that is the ego/intellect and into the rich medium of Consciousness Units that composes your little piece of the Universe. In these dramas, as you are presented your Lessons, you are, in a sense, "forced" to perceive these Issues. It is as though the subconscious, at least for the moment, is helping you to face the music and learn your Lessons.

You are thus challenged to react or to transform. Yet many of you, again, with the aid of denial and intellectualization, sidestep this intervention by finding <u>reasons</u> to account for the dramas. You find reasons for the dramas or you refuse to even consider your contribution. This we call denial. You do have a choice, however, in each instance.

You are finding yourself challenged, therefore, within your area of expertise...

Life-changing Encounter

Let me provide an example. Your Soul Self has set you up to have a life-changing encounter with a teacher of some sort, in your existence. Now this teacher challenges you, let us say, by exhibiting profound and superior information on a particular subject that you know quite well. And suppose that this human also possesses a persuading characteristic that "bothers" you. Perhaps they are charismatic.

Now for my analysis... (humorously) the behavior of this human bothers you because you are perceiving through the perspective of your ego/intellect. You are finding yourself challenged, therefore, within your area of expertise: art, let us say, or perhaps one of the trades. The ego is concerned with appearances, primarily, and so resists any diminishment of its power in these encounters. Indeed, the ego/intellect might often respond by entrenchment, intellectualization, denial, anger, envy, and so on. These emotional states are the common purview of the egoic perspective.

Unfortunately, the life-changing encounter will not be very profound for this subject if they remain entrenched within their limited personal reality manifestation. The continued demonstration by this challenging individual of their superiority, may have the effect of preventing the healing interaction from occurring. Our subject might, indeed, walk away in a huff of self-importance and righteous indignation.

Yet suppose that our subject, a young woman, for example, is on her quest for self-understanding as the result of a recent brush with death, or some other ominous catalyst. She is COMPELLED to look beyond her ego responses to the actions of the human before her, and assess the deeper meanings and opportunities here. Suppose that she has read one of my new books (humorously) and she is involved in living out her Divine Day experimentation. She might well be successful in <u>not</u> succumbing to the forces of negativity, if only briefly. This brief respite from negative Reality Creation may be enough for her to gain some stability in the moment of creation, such that, she could switch her perspective from the ego/intellect to that of the Divine - the Soul Self. The ego is diminished in this moment. The Divine is embodied, invoked, manifested. This new perspective may allow our student example to simply smile and learn from this challenging human. Indeed, she would be learning her Lessons here and contributing to the further evolution of her Soul.

Honor these emotional constructs,
AND THEN transform them…

The Negative Emotions

Now: we are not here suggesting that the student repress, dismiss, or otherwise invalidate these Negative Emotions. We ARE suggesting that the student NOT re-create the negative emotions unnecessarily, until a deep state of negative consciousness is achieved. Anger may become violence if accepted unchecked, unchallenged. Anger if turned inward - into the personal psyche - may fester and cause imbalances of all sorts. Fear may do as much damage, as you may already know.

And so... no, we are not advocating repression of the emotions. Feel the emotions; sense where they are coming from in your experience; honor these emotional constructs; AND THEN transform them by assuming the positive perspective - that of the divine creator All That Is.

They are co-creating their reality intentionally, with divine guidance…

The Benevolent Conspiracy

As you learn your Lessons, consciously or unconsciously, you are aided and abetted by Soul Family members. (humorously) Perhaps you already know of my theory of Soul Family: you incarnate together to learn your Lessons together. Consider the previous example. The challenging expert may well be a Soul Family member learning their Lessons with our subject, the female student on the spiritual path. Yet, suppose that the expert is NOT on a spiritual path of any sort. They are not aware of any subtext of Reincarnational Drama in their interactions with our student.

However, they are still learning their Lessons in this example. They are learning their Lessons by default. Suppose that this expert is arrogant but is continually experiencing opportunities to learn humility, as in our example. The expert has a choice of demeaning our student and learning their Lesson by default - essentially improving their arrogance and avoiding the Lesson of humility - or perhaps acknowledging the communication stream of the Divine within their consciousness. In this case they are relinquishing control, and allowing the higher centers - the higher powers - their involvement. Humility is achieved, thereby, and the expert is no longer learning by default; they are co-creating their reality intentionally, with divine guidance, you might say.

Similarly, for all concerned in this interaction, for all Soul Family members, there exists varying levels of participation in the Reincarnational Drama. Everyone is learning something here, either consciously or by default. In this way, even the simple representation of consciousness manifestation within this interaction between the expert and the student, is imbued with divine importance. For all involved have the opportunity to "do the right thing," and co-create their existence from the divine perspective, for the highest good of all, you see.

*Your ...llect is a function
...elief system...*

Lessons

You are on your Earth to learn a variety of Lessons: some pleasant, some certainly not pleasant, as you perceive it. Thus my reference that it is the human condition that you may very well experience humiliation and ecstatic awakening in successive moments of Reality Creation. The possibilities are limitless within each moment of your existence. Thus my assertion that ALL of created reality is available to you within each moment of co-creating with All That Is.

Everything that can exist, does exist, within the CU. You could say that the CU has this limitless potential to become anything imagined. Yet you ARE experiencing your Lessons. You ARE witnessing the feedback of your mentality that is your Personal Reality, that is, remember, constructed through "instructions," you might say, from your ego/intellect. Your ego/intellect is a function of your belief system. This aspect of your consciousness believes that it is getting a "TRUE" picture of reality as it unconsciously creates the Reincarnational Dramas and comedies of your life.

*Yet many of you do not stop at one
disappointing experience...*

Self-Generated Negativity

Disappointment, frustration, rejection… all of these states of consciousness are self-generated, in that you create your Personal Reality to reflect your inner mentality, with all of its emotions, images, circular thoughts, and so on. Again, it is momentary, in that you create moment-to-moment these enduring states.

"Why, however," you might ask yourself, "do I create these negative states?" Again I remind you, your Issues guide you in the creation of the negative realities. Disappointment, for example, is a very common state of consciousness for many of you, and so it follows that it is a very common negative reality created by many of you. You-the-reader may possibly identify with this state of consciousness, for you have been "disappointed" before in your experiences in physical reality. What does this entail? Simply that your <u>expectations</u> were not met to your satisfaction.

I might suggest that the ego/intellect is running things here, as it often does, and may have "set you up" for disappointment. There is an old saying that applies: "the only thing that pain teaches you is to stop creating pain."

Font size

Yet many of you do not stop at one disappointing experience. You create lifetimes of disappointment.

It would seem obvious, but an objective observer might comment on this tendency to not learn from your mistakes i.e. your unreasonable expectations. The solution here would be to NOT have unreasonable expectations. Learn from your mistakes. Learn your Lessons, Dear Reader. If you find that you are becoming frustrated in your attempts at creating what you desire, fine-tune your Reality Creation strategies to more underlineralistically reflect what it is you want.

We are not suggesting you lower your expectations, but merely adjust them to reflect what is possible for you considering your current experienced reality. Work the "edge" of manifestation, here, and redefine your frustration as "Learning": a Soulful activity.

The Soul sees the truth of your existence;
that all is Love…

The Soul's Perspective

Now what occurs here in the "disappointing" moment is this… your ego/intellect creates a sense of Lack for your having experienced less than was expected. The ego intellect is motivated through the concerns of the personality. The Soul Self, on the other hand, is motivated from an expectation of Love, that is all. The egoic concerns do not concern the Soul Self. The Soul Self does not ever hold unreasonable expectations. The Soul sees the truth of your existence: that all is Love. It is only through the misguided perceptions of the ego/intellect that you, for example, would become disappointed - "depressed" as you say - if you were expecting a lavish birthday cake, and received only a small cookie with a candle in it.

Now seeing through the eyes of the Soul Self, what do you suppose you would see in this gift of the cookie? You would see, from this divine perspective, only Love with a capital L. The gift would be appreciated for the bestowal of Love upon the recipient that it indeed was.

Humility is a very important Lesson
to learn for all of you…

Learning Your Lessons

Suppose you are a fervent practitioner of the Christian faith. This is your perception. You see yourself as a devoted follower, one who practices the spiritual principles expressed by The Christ and others in your Bible. This is how you see yourself… as an ideal, if you will. You are a "Good Christian, a God-fearing Christian," let us say.

However, let me interject here with this observation: you are not... none of you are perfect. You all have Lessons to learn. And so our example has a blind spot, let us say, in their character that prevents them from seeing the variances from Christian practices they display in almost every moment of existence. Humility is absent from the consciousness of this human example. They look down on others they assess as not being Christian, or not their type of Christian. They place themselves <u>above</u> others on a regular basis, then, in the search for how they "measure up" to others in the spiritual domain.

Humility is a very important Lesson to learn for all of you. The religious practitioner who avoids the Lesson of humility is doing more harm than good. They are setting themselves up for another incarnational journey with the Lesson of humility paramount on the agenda. This is how it is for Souls experiencing human form upon your world.

You are now acting out your emotional drama…

Habitual Ways of Reacting

Obviously, for many of you, your emotional reactions are automatic. You experience something that "upsets" you, offends you in some way, let us say, and you automatically launch into an overt negative reaction. For example, you become "hot under the collar," and "storm around the house," re-creating automatically the negative emotional state. Let us call it anger or righteous indignation in this example. Someone or thing has "pushed your buttons," and you are now acting-out your emotional drama on the stage of your existence.

At these times of passion it is good to remember that your automatic responses are simply <u>habitual</u> ways of re-acting. Over your life you have learned – from family and friends – "typical" demonstrations of emotion. You have practiced re-creating these gestures and emotional states whenever you get an opportunity (humorously), and now you have become a master. The process has become habitual, automatic.

Fortunately, habits may be changed over time. We have proposed many interventions for you in my new books. Here let us present a simple antidote to the re-creation of righteous indignation in the moment of your personal consciousness manifestation.

Technique: A Message From Your Higher Self

This is a very simple technique here and we have covered it before. I believe you will have limitless opportunities to practice it in your waking reality. (humorously)

Suppose that you ARE experiencing righteous indignation. You are using the research capabilities of the ego/intellect to re-create anger in your present moments. You are automatically finding reasons to be angry, and perhaps at the same time, denying thoughts and images that come to mind that refute your own negative assessment! Denial and intellectualization are occurring simultaneously, as they often do.

With this technique you divert your attention to the incoming message from your Higher Self. It is always the same message... "Love." " All is well in your world." "Courageously Love others," that type of thing. Allow the incoming message to "color" your Reality Creation strategy in the moment. Anticipate a positive outcome and then simply repeat as needed.

As you continually interject the new adaptation in your opportunities to re-create righteous indignation, you will find that, over time, you learn how to create Loving Understanding in these moments.

*These words acted as a dramatic script
for our example throughout her life...*

The Positive Manifestation

There are Lessons of a Positive nature also for the Reality Creator. We often speak of the Positive Manifestation as it pertains to The Shift in consciousness for humanity. Your positive input fuels The Shift, quite literally. Now what of the Positive Manifestation within the Personal Reality Field of the individual? An example for your further understanding…

Consider the human engaged in creating prosperity for themselves and their family. Let us say that this group was previously "doing without," for the most part. They were without the necessities of existence and were suffering Lack. Then it dawned upon the consciousness of our example - a woman - that she was sabotaging her financial growth subconsciously by obeying self-limiting scripts created in her youth. She was told as a child that she was incapable of creating anything of value, for she was a "natural born loser." She was told by her parents that she "destroyed everything she touched."

Now these words acted as a dramatic script for our example throughout her life. Her parents knew what they were talking about, she assumed, and so she created a life of failure to corroborate her parent's assessment of her. The script became subconscious over time, until now, as an adult, she wonders if she may be cursed. She wonders why her projects seem doomed to fail.

Then the example becomes aware of the momentary thoughts, images, and emotions within her consciousness. She identifies a common thread: "you are a born loser," and rather than continue to accept that, she challenges it within her own experience. She proclaims to herself that she is a natural healer and has successfully facilitated the return to health with many friends over the years. She is successful in this area of her life. Perhaps she may transpose the positive states of consciousness she is experiencing when she is successful in healing to the task of creating prosperity. She discovers that she does have a circular thought that is common to her states of consciousness while being successful. The thought is a statement: "I can do this if I keep at it." This thought fills her with motivation and positive emotion.

By noticing in her self-assessments in the moments of her waking reality, when and where she is creating through the internalized statement/belief that she is a born loser, she is able to respond to this negative assertion with her own positive statement: "I can do this if I just keep at it." Over time, the negative belief is replaced by the positive assertion through the "habit" of ritually replacing the negative thought. Soon the example is experiencing an improved reality in the financial realm.

Experiment - Integrating the Negative Persona
Hypothesis: you can reclaim and integrate the cumulative castoff aspects of soul

Perform Your Ritual of Sanctuary
I trust that you are convinced now that your mission in physical reality is to transform the negative into the positive, (humorously) after first of course,

analyzing the negative manifestation for origins, value, etc. Now when this is done consistently - habitually - there comes a time when the architect of these negative reality constructions becomes quite known to you. This aspect of your consciousness we refer to as the Negative Persona.

We identify it as a subject in order to study this subject. It remains the ultimate truth of your reality that you are complete and utterly whole, un-fragmented, good, and of sacred value unto yourself. However, let us examine this theorized Negative Persona here in an effort of self-understanding and propose an exercise to identify it completely, and then accept it into the consciousness in a ritualized fashion. This will be an "owning" of the personalized negative aspects of consciousness.

Now, as you wrestle with your Lessons, the theorized Negative Persona is created. In your personal underworld it can gain great power, over time, as the uncomfortable aspects of your personality are noticed by the ego/intellect and then intentionally ignored. The perceived negative is a personal opinion, therefore, and this evolving Negative Persona bears the characteristics of human existence that are thought of as shameful, inappropriate, fearful, and so on.

Each human is different in their respective creations of this aspect of consciousness. And because it is such a personal and intimate portrayal by the individual of everything that is perceived as "wrong" about them, it gains a certain treacherous and even potentially catastrophic potential. It is as though you feel that if this information ever comes to light - revealed to family, friends, colleagues - that you would not be able to bear it. You would be destroyed. You would possibly cease to exist.

This is that mythological "beast within" that seeks acknowledgment by the self, but seldom is granted this acknowledgment. Currently, because great numbers of you are awakening in your timeframe, it is necessary for you to "take your medicine," in a sense, with regards to acknowledging this Negative Persona. All of you are in your Issues at this time. All of you are deep within your Lessons. All of you are being called upon to accept responsibility for your negative selves, so that you will cease projecting your disavowed aspects of self onto others: mates, families, nations, collectives of all types.

Your Negative Persona is best recognized in the negative remarks made to you by others concerning your personality and behavior. To be sure, some of these comments may have intrinsic value: they may be quite true, in other words. Your task is to determine the truth in these negative comments and own these comments. Take responsibility here. Then as you assess the negative comments that do not pertain to you, but were perhaps mere projections of fear and doubt from your friends and family, get a sense of this collective persona.

♦ How does it feel to confront this aspect of your personality?
♦ Is there a sense of familiarity here, as though you have been aware of this element, but were perhaps afraid to fully face it?

Now simply acknowledge this construct as a very important part of you, the other side of you, in fact. This is to be done with Courage and Loving Understanding as your primary operating perspective.

Findings: Please document your Findings

_____
_____
_____
_____
_____

ACT THREE

(Conscious Co-creation)

Conscious co-creation entails the intentional learning of Lessons. The Lessons of physical existence are not denied nor are they intellectualized. This is also what you call Enlightenment or Soul Evolution.

CONSCIOUS
CO-CREATION

Loving co-creation is god-building…

Conscious Co-creation is Awakening

For each second that you are consciously co–creating a Loving reality, you are also awakening in the spiritual sense; you are awakening to your Higher Self. Now, for each second that you re-create fear and anger you are being controlled by the negative Gestalts of Consciousness. Thus we have this simple dynamic that I have described for you before: Loving co-creation is god-building; the re-creation of anxiety, fear, anger and cynicism supports the Negative Entities. These Entities are the negative gods of your religious systems.

You see, each of you reacts differently - in a personalized manner - when you encounter the negative emotions. It is true that the emotional states of the human are easily recognizable, broadly speaking, in that an observer could easily surmise what are the emotional states currently of those before them. However, the internal manifestation of the emotional state is colored by characteristics of personality and individual temperament. It is in this arena of the personal consciousness of the individual where the "decision" is made to either meet and transform the emotional state or to re-create it without thoughtful input – subconsciously, you see.

In this realm of perception is where the student gains their findings in the exploratory venture as a Scientist of Consciousness. YOUR consciousness is the laboratory here, to continue our quaint little metaphor. Your unswerving crystal-clear focus on the phenomena within your "mind" represents the requisite objective critical thinking aspect of the scientist: the empirical perspective. We are referring in this section to our two books from our last series, in which we outlined the path for the Scientist of Consciousness and made our case for the necessity of this approach at this critical time in your history.

*Here then, your perspective and my
perspective are identical…*

From my Perspective

I often use the phrase in these new manuscripts, "from my perspective." Let me speak a bit about what that might mean. Now please remember, here in our discussions it is perception that <u>causes</u> Reality Creation. The Percept, as we have defined it in our book ***Thought Reality***, is that aspect of consciousness that simultaneously and instantaneously creates and perceives the Reality Construct. Therefore, can you <u>see</u> that from my perspective I <u>am witness to</u> your greater multidimensional experiencing? This enlarged perspective of mine includes the goings-on within your probable futures.

The mind reels here in contemplation of this perspective. However, if you are with us on this voyage, and you are attending to exercises and experimentation we present to you, I would suggest that your mind may now be in the beginning stages of a new stability with regards to <u>witnessing</u> the multidimensional nature of the self that is quite commonplace to Light Beings.

That is what it is all about, this shift to 4th-Dimensional Awareness. From my perspective, many of you are becoming quite expert at "holding" this state of awareness for extended periods of time. Here then, your perspective and my perspective are identical. We are on the same wavelength, in a very literal way. We are focused on this same compelling subject of interest. We are all of us witnessing the divine creation of realities moment-to-moment.

*The small awakenings foreshadow the full
awakening experience...*

A Message From the Entity

Currently the episodes are necessarily brief - fractions of a second in length - to allow your ego-consciousness to remain focused in the Third Dimension. But you are now awakening, you are now in the midst of The Shift. Your capacities, therefore, for understanding are increasing. Your Inner Senses are becoming quite acute. Your skills at turning the negative into the positive are sharpening. For these reasons, your Holographic Inserts will intensify - in so far as sensory data is concerned - and lengthen in linear time.

The visions - perceptions of the visionary - are the HIs experienced in depth. These messages from yourself, from your future selves, from your awakened progressed consciousness, will become for you the common day-to-day experiencing in your current existence. In this way, the small awakenings foreshadow the full awakening experience that awaits you when you are ready.

You are simply anticipating a response, here...

Effects of The Shift

Several years ago we predicted that soon great numbers of you would be empowered to use the multitasking "feature" of your awakening consciousness. We stated that it would be commonplace for you, in the middle of a conversation with your peers or family members, to pause and receive incoming information from your Higher Self. You would then resume your conversation and possibly incorporate the material you received from your Higher Self into your narrative. If this is the case with you, Dear Reader, please take just a few seconds to pause in your reading, and open up to messages from your Higher Self. You are simply anticipating a response, here. Do not try to figure it out. Just relax and be open to what you are experiencing...

Please allow me to make my point here about being receptive to your higher centers, while referring to an incident that occurred in Mark's backyard. The experience of attempting to free the deer from his back yard may serve as an example of how NOT to interact with Mother Nature or All That Is. Now for the record... (humorously)

Mark panicked when he saw a trapped deer run into the deer fence several times in his back yard. He feared that the animal would possibly kill itself in the panic of attempting to escape. Mark spontaneously called out in anger, further frightening the deer and sending it into a panic of escape.

Let us imagine a different intervention, then, for this example. Suppose that Mark had projected Loving Understanding at the animal, asserting his solidarity with the animal kingdom and with all of Nature. If he were to have assumed a placid neutral demeanor and coaxed the animal toward the opened gate by which it had entered, the deer may have not panicked so dramatically and scaled the fence to escape.

As it was, the deer escaped uninjured. It could have been much worse, however, with Mark experiencing a tragedy in which he participated. Now here, the proof is in the pudding, to coin a phrase. In the heat of the moment, when anger is making itself known, when frustration, fear and anxiety threaten to overwhelm your Reality Creation, that is precisely when you intervene with your thoughts of composure, Loving Understanding, Courage, and so on.

Here you already know how to create anger and act upon it. You are an expert, Mark, as are many of you in physical reality. (humorously) The trick is to GO BEYOND the old ways of thinking, emoting, and behaving. Indeed, the idea is, after having taken responsibility for the creation of the reality, to do the opposite with regards to thinking, emoting, behaving. It all occurs in the moment, Dear Reader. In the heat of the moment is when you learn these valuable Lessons.

You are allowing the Soul's perspective
to predominate…

The Shift is a Birthing Phenomenon

In our new books we have given you many words of explanation regarding the Fourth-Dimensional Shift. This transformative period in which you find yourselves, as a species and as a world, comes at the end of a long evolutionary cycle in physical reality. Many hundreds of thousands of years of consciousness manifestation have brought you here to the doorstep of a great awakening for humanity. We call it "consciousness becoming aware of itself, ultimately, to the nth degree." Evolutionary consciousness, or All That Is, has reached a culmination in the reality of the Third Dimension.

For practical purposes, for you-the-reader, this Shift is having great effects on your Personal Reality as we speak. Undoubtedly you are "in your issues" with regards to the learning of your individual Lessons. So you do indeed know what I am speaking of here with The Shift, in so far as your personal relationship to it is concerned.

Now here is where your ego/intellect most probably will defend itself with "reasons" and "proofs" that you are different from the rest. You have no Lessons to learn. You are doing quite well and do not need personal critiques from someone who doesn't even know you, from a discarnate being, no less. This we call intellectualization and denial in our manuscripts. It is a normal response to these perceived allegations we proffer to the reader on a continuing basis.

However, if you continue to read the books, you ARE looking for something of value, even as you somewhat deny the worth of these messages. So gradually you are making your way at your own pace, Dear Reader. You are opening up slowly, on your own schedule. You are allowing the Soul's perspective to predominate in your Reality Creation activities rather than the perspective of the ego/intellect.

There is certainly as much aggression and "thrust"
within the feminine component...

The Birthing of the New World

Now your Earth is an entity unto herself. You call your world the Mother Earth, ascribing to this planet the feminine, nurturing qualities of life. However, there is also the counterpart to the feminine inherent in each atom of your physical existence. I have described to you before how this interplay of electromagnetic energies - the perceived opposites - serves to "light and power" your Reality Constructs. And so in our descriptions of the creation phenomenon, particularly with regards to the ascendance of the New World via the 4th-Dimensional Shift, we include and indeed <u>honor</u> the counter energies of manifestation.

For your better understanding, you might say that it is the feminine, nurturing, generative aspects of All That Is that serve to energize and support this thrust of physical reality into your system. The interested reader may reference my earlier works for discussions of ***natural aggression*** to further their understanding here of this phenomenon.

Still let us present our disclaimer, as we must: there is certainly as much aggression and "thrust" within the feminine component of manifestation as in the so-called masculine. We are attempting to offer you simple descriptions of these deep issues so that you may grasp the meaning of the divine construct - Reality Creation.

Thus, in this birthing of the New World, all of you are playing your parts. You are created from consciousness through the same process of manifestation as any other Reality Construct. If it helps, you could think of your Personal Reality Field as a reflection of your Inner Self, your Soul Self. The entire Universe, including your Mother Earth, is a projection from the Inner Self or Logos of All That Is. And so on, and so on, you see, down to the Personal Reality of an atom, for example, as it perceives its theoretical electrons spinning around it. And so on, even

further still, as far in   you would like to take this
introspection: infinitely, if you have the patience.

> *All values are fulfilled instantaneously*
> *in the spacious moment of creation…*

Projections of Consciousness

We will now add to the material we have covered on
projections. In this metaphor we maintain that All That is
- which includes everything in your created reality including you, Dear Reader - projects itself, its essence, if you
will, into the Third Dimension. What results in this projection are Reality Constructs of all types. In a way, as
you project your Personal Reality Field into 3D Reality of
Earth from within, you are responding to All That Is as it
seeks Value Fulfillment in the creation of, again, all types
of Reality Constructs. It all happens at once. All values
are fulfilled instantaneously in the spacious moment of
creation.

So from the this perspective it has many advantages
for the student. For example: you may see the end results
of any proposed Reality Creation agenda you might be
considering. In the divine perspective of All That Is, there
is no lag-time in the manifestation of realities, as you experience it.

This divine perspective can be yours if you wish. By
embodying the Divine you gain a perspective that lies out-

side of linear time in the eternal moment. You needn't wait for any proposed agenda to be implemented and experienced over days, weeks, or months, let us say. You would know instantly the outcomes of your proposed "projects" for Reality Creation.

These templates of creation are limitless...

With Whose Eyes?

In this little essay we shall explore the concept of the human embodying certain perspectives, and so creating their realities through these blueprints, or Gestalts of Consciousness. Now you literally have at your disposal access to <u>unlimited</u> perspectives or Gestalts of Consciousness, that you may embody, ally with, and proceed to create your world in tandem, you might say, with another consciousness manifestation. These templates of creation are limitless, for they include the varied aspects of personality embodied by humans over the millennia. These ways of behaving, of feeling, of thinking, and imagining exist within your collective consciousness as a reservoir of potential Reality Creation energy to which you may turn in your many existences.

Thus, for example, you might be a human engaged in creating a life for yourself in your ancient Egyptian era, perhaps as a slave. Many of you have done and are cur-

rently doing just that   ou imagine how fantastically
different is the self-c   istence of our Egyptian friend
we are discussing, to the life you-the-reader are currently
creating for yourself? Utterly and completely different, I'm
certain you would agree. For the ancient one is working
from the perspective of a slave living in an ancient culture
within a totally different confluence of influences - the
social, religious, and others - than you, Dear Reader. This
human is observing through their unique vision, their world:
the Personal Reality Field.

Let us take this further on the assumption that what I
am telling you here is quiet true: that you are all living
lives as slaves in some of your Reincarnational Existences,
even though you may be currently reading this manuscript
through the eyes of a typical modern human, one who has
access to all of the modern conveniences, one who is relatively free, and so on.

Some of my readers may now be seeing where I am
taking this discussion. Let me continue. All That Is is the
creative medium in which consciousness, through physical form, expresses itself. These expressions include the
physical bodies and existences of all of your Simultaneous Lives. ALL OF EXISTENCE occurs simultaneously, in the present moment - the spacious moment,
as we also call it.

Do you see how it is possible for you to <u>embody</u> this timeless perspective here and now, allowing your current experiencing consciousness to tune-in to the other life lived as perhaps an Egyptian slave? You are already doing so, however you are probably not yet proficient in the multi-tasking necessary to retain the memories of your other lives. Practice is necessary here. Practice until you can remember.

Gradually you gain some control
over these bleedthroughs...

Negative Bleedthroughs

You may at this time be sensing bleedthroughs from some of these lives in which you are experiencing negative emotional states. I have discussed this briefly in my books of decades ago. The bleedthroughs begin spontaneously without any foreshadowing. The emotional material, at first, is difficult to assess. One moment you may be in quite good spirits, and the next moment, though nothing has changed in your current existence, you are in quite low spirits. Your current mental environment has been contaminated by the past-life negative emotions.

It would be advantageous at these times to bring in your Sanctuary and protect your consciousness from further encroachment. Over time, using this Sanctuary as a protective mechanism, the spontaneous connections to the negative past lives occur less often. Gradually you gain some control over these bleedthroughs, so that you can experience them on your terms.

For example: this type of information from your other lives may be necessary for your continued growth. Facing the negative aspects of your greater self may be a part of your awakening experience. Exploring these past-life sources of current negative experiencing may help you to achieve control in other areas of your life.

Their vision is a dark one, you see...

The 2012 Phenomenon

The visionary state to which you aspire is always available to you. This state of consciousness exists in probability at all times, for the time is right for this ascension of human consciousness. In your popular media you can see this. The 2012 phenomenon is exhibited for you in your books and other media, as a potentially horrendous affair entailing the destruction of the planet and humanity. These are actually the collective fears of humans being given life by authors, directors, and other artists. Their vision is a dark one, you see. They are going for the sensationalist expression of the potential inherent in this great change that lies before you.

Yet, the opposite is also true here. The changes that you will experience in the coming years have just as much potential to express in positive ways as in the negative. Indeed, you could say that our visionary exercises are specifically tuned to allow a perception of this positive outcome, what we call the Positive Collective Manifestation. In my books I presented an exercise for the researcher that wishes to explore this collective manifestation as it creates itself out of the positive thoughts, emotions, images, and beliefs of humanity.

Here I will present an exercise that you may carry with you so that you may become an advocate: an ongoing contributor to this Positive Manifestation.

Indeed, they are the ground upon which they stand as well as the entire Earth itself...

Technique: Sensing the Positive Manifestation

We are assuming that you have perfected the Ritual of Sanctuary somewhat, so that you may take your state of Sanctuary with you, from your home into the world at large. If you have not yet perfected this technique, please do so before attempting this exercise. The Ritual of Sanctuary may be found at the end of this book.

This exercise assumes you are in your protected state of Sanctuary out in the marketplace, in nature, in your workplace, or any other location outside of your normal living quarters.

~~~~~

The collective manifestation is continually being created from the subconscious status quo contributions of humans in the collective. In this way, the status quo reality is kept intact moment-to-moment. You will not see any great changes, therefore, in the day-to-day manifestation of your waking world. You agree as a collective, while you sleep, what will be created on awakening from sleep. When you wake-up you immediately go about creating the consensus reality subconsciously, along the lines agreed on during sleep. However, because you are gaining a facility with creating the state of Sanctuary and carrying it with you, it is possible for you to experience the inner world of consensus Reality Creation while still maintaining contact with Third-Dimensional reality: a foot in both worlds, we say in the new material.

~~~~~

To attain the visionary state at-will is to embody All That Is at-will. We have spoken before of the researcher becoming Mother Earth by embodying Mother Earth. At these times the researcher feels quite grounded. Indeed, they are the ground upon which they stand as well as the entire Earth itself – Mother Earth. Here it is the same concept. You embody All That Is to gain the visionary perspective. Having assumed the perspective of All That Is, you may then approach the Positive Consensus Manifestation realm. Simply turning your attention inwards, toward the Soul, you might say.

~~~~~

You will be creating a light Trance for yourself. Anything deeper than this may be inappropriate for you as you experience your waking reality. Physical safety issues come into play here when you are experimenting in your community. Therefore, with an eye toward you personal safety, having already conducted your Ritual of Sanctuary, consider, with the eyes open now, your visualized route to the realm of the Positive Manifestation for humanity.

~~~~~

The markers along the way on this visualized quest have positive emotion attached to them. These indicators will be personal to you and you alone, according to your orientation: visual, auditory, tactile, olfactory, and so on. The Inner Senses will guide you to your destination if you will allow them to. When you feel as though you are making contact with this realm make your mental contribution - an empowered thought, image, or emotion - and then return to surface awareness.

You are now experiencing bleedthroughs
to your other existences...

The Epiphany

You are the visionary. The vision you will perceive is wholly dependent upon your personal experiences, your thoughts, the images you have within your consciousness at any one time. It is a very personal thing, then, this vision. It is in truth an intimate portrayal of your momentary spiritual awakening.

We have said that the vision is often quite brief: a fraction of a second, usually. However, because these events exist outside of time for the most part, you may return to these visionary experiences and witness them in their full sustained glory. You do this in the Trance state or the meditative state, of course, in a ritual fashion. Using your Intent you revisit the visionary glimpse and you focus upon the various aspects of the event.

For example: suppose you are going about your business in your waking existence, and you quite suddenly have a powerful, yet brief epiphany, as you call it. Let us say that previously you were perplexed about the actions and hurtful behaviors of a loved-one. Now suppose that this loved-one "acted out of character," and was intentionally cruel to you. You have been wondering why for many days or weeks. Then it occurs to you: because you are a researcher of your personal reality, and because you are now experiencing bleedthroughs to your other existences, you are finding correlations between the issues and Lessons of your current existence and those Lessons you are learning in other existences, in your perceived past, let us say.

Now this will seem outrageous to those of you who are not doing the work in these books of mine. Please bear with us…

The subtext of the reincarnational drama: the hidden meaning, in other words…

Past-Life Payback

Suppose that, because you have found a similarity of behavior in a loved one from this past existence and the behavior of your current loved one, you are therefore receiving more information - background information, quite literally - concerning your current existence and the current problematic loved one. This we also call the subtext, as in the subtext of the reincarnational drama: the hidden meaning, in other words.

With this new information a threshold of understanding is reached subconsciously. Suppose you have a brief glimpse into your past-life and witness the counterpart to your current loved one experiencing harm at your hand. This could indeed be violent harm directed at this loved one from another life, by you in your past-life body, your Simultaneous Life.

Now in your current existence you are using an entirely different body than in the past and the human that you abused in the past-life is inhabiting the body of the loved one that has been intentionally cruel to you for no apparent reason. Yet now, after the epiphany, the moment of increased understanding, you have an apparent "cause" of the intentionally cruel behavior. This may be "pay back," in a sense, in response to a relatively innocuous perceived slight experienced by the loved one in question. The loved one is responding to a much greater slight received AT YOUR HAND in the past-life.

The epiphany is quite productive and healing, here, if you take the time to meditate on it. It may allow you to take this behavior with a grain of salt, as you say. Yes, they are over-reacting currently. However, in the past-life experience, YOU were the perpetrator of much greater abuse on this loved one. It is an opportunity, therefore, to not react with anger and fear but with Loving Understanding and Courage, having seen the bigger picture.

*You are spirit, my friend. You are composed
of spiritual material...*

Suggestions Clarifications and So On

This next section may contain material unsuitable for my older readers. (humorously) These subjects were not discussed in earlier works with Jane Roberts and her husband. They believed such discussions were "unscientific," in that, to their minds, ideas of gods and goddesses, spiritual hierarchies, and so on, merely illustrated how the human consciousness may "personalize" the creative energies of All That Is. We are having this discussion now, for I see that these issues have been neglected in studies of my works, in your books, on your Internet, and in other media.

Now: you are Spirit, my friend; you are composed of spiritual material. Whether you wish to use your helpful metaphor of the atomic structure of Reality Constructs, or my metaphor of the Consciousness Units, at the "beginning" of your self-created reality, including your body, is Spirit. You are an etheric being first and foremost, then.

I do realize that some of you may not wish to focus on this aspect, though you may grudgingly admit your spiritual basis. You may have a fear of being carried away on these far-out theories, to a place where you may be, shall we say, coerced into taking on a particular set of beliefs, as in the missionary efforts of the world religions. I assure you that is not my intention here. In actuality, I encourage those of our readers who practice the tenets of the various religious faiths, to simply use our information that we offer as suggestions, clarifications, and so on.

Your world is created in this current moment by spiritual beings of great power...

The Spiritual Hierarchy

Let us describe the Hierarchy for you as an example of Gestalts of Consciousness, the etheric basis of the physical world. That is to say, every physical construct, every atom, molecule of air, every tree, human or insect has its origination in the etheric - the nonphysical world. If you are familiar with my new works, you well know that I attribute even systems of reality such as your medical model, as having emerged from these complex etheric structures of propensity.

To you, as a human existing within your specific coordinates of time and space - your linear time continuum - it appears that, for example, the world religions "grew" out of their separate foundational events. And if you are religiously-minded, that God, for example, was the literal creator of your Earth, most certainly, as well as the chief propagator and inspiration for the growth of these movements. This is how it looks inside the linear time illusion, with the basic assumption of cause-and-effect.

Consider now, however, the truth of the matter. If you are with us here on the spontaneous and simultaneous nature of Earthly existence, you may be able now to grasp this assertion of mine with your intuitive understanding, rather than the logical intellect...

Your world is created in this current moment by spiritual beings of great power. For our purposes, we refer to the creators as the Spiritual Hierarchy, yet you too, as a Reality Creator, have your place here in this timeless moment of creation. You could even quite correctly assume that you are this Spiritual Hierarchy of world creators in the physical world, as they, as Bodies of Light, represent your interests in the etheric world.

Yes, you are you, Dear Reader, as you read the words on this page or hear the spoken narrative, even as you are these evolved masters of creation, the members of the Spiritual Hierarchy. Previously we have noted that, as a reader of my works, you ally with the Seth Entity. You give the Seth Entity energy in this exchange, just as the Seth Entity gives you energy. In a similar way, the masters of the Spiritual Hierarchy are informed, energized, and enlightened by your input, just as you may become so through the exchange of energies. In reading these works, in experiencing the Holographic Inserts I am transmitting to your consciousness, in opening yourself up to these benevolent communication streams, you are changed.

Again, fears of being drawn into an unwanted cultish relationship, may serve to repel the Holographic Inserts. However, if you are focused on your studies, it is possible to transform the fear. Transform it into Courage, then move on with your investigations.

This personalization process serves a purpose
for the individual explorer…

Personalizing the Divine Energies

This assemblage of masters, the Spiritual Hierarchy, do have names and have been identified by visionaries throughout your history. This is the personalization that takes place naturally in the human participation in divine perception. However, for our purposes, we will not go into the endless lists of names given to the Light Bodies. We are keeping it simple for you here, and direct you to your own experiments for the names of these beings.

Thus, if you were to attempt contact with the divine beings, and you were sincere and focused, you would quite probably discover your own pantheon of gods and goddesses. You might obtain names for the divine beings that are unlike any others obtained by spiritual investigators in your perceived past. Yet I am certain that if you were to compare the Inner Senses assessments of the beings with descriptions from, let us say, your Christian bible, or the Koran, or the Buddhist texts, you would find that, though the names differ, the Light Bodies are indeed the same throughout all investigations into their origins by human explorers. This personalization process serves a purpose for the individual explorer of the personal reality. It gives them "something to work with," as they conduct their experiments: i.e. the ritual search for the Divine.

It is often only on the deathbed that the disbeliever finds how very wrong they were...

God

In our book **Thought Reality** we gave the reader a preview of this current manuscript. In that discussion we spoke of the "folly" of believing in the <u>death</u> of God. In my first manuscripts done with Jane and her husband, you can sense this thoughtform that was entertained by great numbers of you. You in the West were looking for something more, something less religious, something more easily grasped, I suppose.

The irony in this statement - God is dead - is that it is often only on the deathbed that the disbeliever finds how very wrong they were. The ego/intellect dissolves abruptly during the Transition revealing only the Soul's perspective. This perspective sees no duality with relation to the

Divine. The Soul knows that it IS eternal, it is NOT separate, it IS both a part of and the complete whole of All That Is.

It is unfortunate that many, perhaps out of fear of being perceived as "weak" or perhaps "mentally challenged," do not go on that inner journey. To these humans it is a surprise that they ARE God, they ARE eternal, they are NOT dying, but merely transforming their energy into something else.

You are centered within All That Is...

The Graphic Representation

All That Is represents in physical reality, the collective mentalities and energies of all forms on Earth and including the very Earth itself. We have stated before that there is no beginning nor any ending to your Universe. There is only the present moment of creation in which All creates All That Is.

You live under a necessary assumption of linear time and cause-and-effect, and so you take it for granted that everything has a beginning and ending. This assumption, however, when brought to an attempted understanding of spiritual concerns, can lead to mis-perceptions and confusion. We encourage the reader to momentarily abandon these preconceived notions and root assumptions as we attempt to further illustrate the truth of the matter. For when you can, even for the moment, release your hold on physical reality, and experience the timeless moment of the NOW, you automatically gain a more truthful perspective of your reality.

When you let go, when you go with the flow of creation in the moment, you are centered within All That Is and you are participating as a co-creator with this Loving force. As many of you at the same moment in linear time, for example, conduct this experiment, you as a collective of researchers create a subgroup from all of humanity, whose focus in those moments is the re-creation of Love with a capital L.

As you, perhaps at the time each day, conduct your investigations, a tendency is created within the greater collective of which your subgroup is a part, to defer to the positive Loving manifestation, rather than the mundane or the negative manifestations. This is the resonance phenomenon in action, if you care to identify it. This process of Loving your Earth through this multitude of subgroups composed of visionaries, will be the critical factor in The Shift you are experiencing.

The "strength in numbers" phenomenon is demonstrated here as well. The Positive Manifestation is reaching the tipping point of inevitability, you see. I sense that you are receiving the messages I am attempting to convey.

*The churches and the religions will become
more democratic...*

Religious Authority

You have systematically over the generations given away your creative powers to those in perceived authority. Of these authorities the religious authority is perhaps the most powerful. It is not uncommon, for example, on your Sunday observances, for millions of humans to engage in the obedience to religious authority. See what occurs in your communities in the Christian nations during your religious holidays. Whole peoples are seen enacting rituals of the holidays, celebrating the life of The Christ.

Now where here does the authority lie? Primarily, as the intermediary between humanity and the Divine, it is with the priest first, and then the members of the church hierarchy. The officials are entrusted with the powers of creation given by the practitioners.

Now we have spoken elsewhere of the necessity in this time of awakening, to rethink these power exchanges that the individual has with the intermediaries of the Divine. As this occurs, and many of you begin to take back your power from religious figures, the churches and the religions will become more democratic. They will become humanized. The rituals will be transformed into more truthful demonstrations of the manifestation process.

Finally you are experiencing
the visionary perspective...

Inflated Ego/intellect

You are awakening at this time. As you sharpen your Inner Senses and remember what we are calling the Ancient Wisdom, it may begin to occur to you that you are becoming quite powerful indeed. As you gain control over your Reality Creation energies, and you become a conscious co-creator with All That Is, the ego/intellect naturally becomes elevated at times, such that you may begin to feel superior to those around you. This emotional state you might call egotistical..

The following experiment is simply a focused application of our very basic technique of transforming the negative emotions into their divine opposites. Here we are assuming that some progress has been made in your visionary experiencing. You are getting brief glimpses of what you may call the Divine. This success may have come after many, many attempts to break through this veil that separates you from your greater consciousness expression. Naturally you would feel satisfaction. Finally you are seeing the value in these arcane practices. At last you are introduced to your guidance. Finally you are experiencing the visionary perspective, at least, perhaps, for a few moments in your waking day.

Now we have stated that after the preliminary steps are taken by the student, there is a momentum that is achieved, such that your results multiply in rapid fashion. What is occurring for you here is the natural habitual creation of the visionary state. Through your ritual practices of these techniques, you have made the visionary state habitual, so that you need only practice your techniques briefly before you encounter substantial results. You are mastering the work.

There is the accompanying element of ecstasy in these studies that keeps you moving forward. Indeed, you are induced to continue with your contact and communications with the Divine until a final enlightening episode that is charged with the ecstatic emotions occurs.

Yet, what occurs when you are finished with your experiments for the day and you are at your job, or out in the field in your mundane existence? There may be a tendency to become quite "full of yourself" as the ego/intellect takes credit for these positive rewards. Within all spiritual practices the shrewd discerning student may identify those practitioners that have successfully achieved a spiritual awakening, yet have lost their gratitude and humility along the way. To avoid this pitfall on the path of awakening, we offer the following experiment.

Experiment - Polarizing the inflated ego/intellect
Hypothesis: by embodying the opposite of the inflated ego/intellect humility is achieved

Perform Your Ritual of Sanctuary

We have spoken in our books on the value of a concept we call "the humble god or goddess." The basis here is Love with a capital L. This Love is pervasive: for oneself, for others, also. Love predominates in all of your interactions.

Yet in this description lies an inherent dichotomy, for the humble human is also charismatic. The lover of humanity is a beacon to others. It is quite attractive this humility of spirit. To manifest both charisma and humility is the mark of the self-realized, the enlightened, the awakened ones.

Now polarizing means <u>embodying the opposite</u> of the identified emotional state. You intentionally live the opposite of, for example, the egotistical state. The opposite might be described as a state of humility. Thus, you would visualize yourself as the humble one, and all that it might entail. Imagine how that would feel. Imagine your specific behaviors as the humble one and then embody them. Act them out in your waking reality.

During this experiment it may dawn on you that you are also polarizing your state of humility. The opposite of a state of humble awareness you might call charisma. In this way, you are holding together the poles of human emotion. Within the two extremes there exists a broad field of emotional experiencing for the awakening human.

Findings: Please document your Findings

_____

_____

_____

_____

_____

EPILOGUE

All That Is
The Holographic Insert

I trust you have found something of value in our little book of essays. Certainly we have not explored the subject definitively. However, the complete expression of All That Is <u>can</u> be sensed inwardly as a Holographic Insert. Therefore, I now place this Idea Construct within these words. You may access this message at any time. Use your intent to guide your Inner Senses to the precise location within your mental environment. This construct has ecstatic emotion attached to it. This emotion will intensify as you approach it. You will know you have made contact when your emotional state becomes transformed to the positive. This is awakening, Dear Reader. Good luck with your studies.

THE END

RITUAL OF SANCTUARY

The Ritual of Sanctuary was presented to readers in our book on Soul Evolution when we first began to emphasize direct exploration of the Unknown Reality. We felt that the reader would require some personalized protection in their experimentation.

The most simple form of the Ritual is to imagine, prior to psychic pursuits, a golden Light surrounding you. Nothing harmful can penetrate this field of Light. It has a healing protective influence. You may certainly use this simplified form while you go about creating your own Ritual.

The object here is to generate positive energies with your creative consciousness. Try listing on a piece of paper your positive beliefs and ideas that denote security, peace, and protection. The next step would be to, perhaps artistically, distill these potent concepts down into an image, statement, or physical object that resonates with the protective energies. Naturally you may include gestures, visualizations, or any other evocative materials. Practice your Ritual until you can create at-will the state of Sanctuary within your own consciousness. Only you will know when you are successful.

Glossary
Definitions for the concepts Seth discusses
in this book.

All That Is - The energy source from which all life sprung throughout the multitude of Universes, transcending all dimensions of consciousness and being part of all. Also referred to as the Logos and Evolutionary Consciousness.

Ancient Wisdom - The knowledge of the magicians, shamans, witches and healers of the past.

Awakening - As the Ancient Wisdom is remembered by humanity, an awareness of the greater reality is experienced by individuals.

Beliefs - Ideas, images, and emotions within your mental environment that act as filters and norms in the creation of Personal Realities.

Bleedthroughs - Momentary experiencing of lives being lived in other tirmeframes and other systems of reality.

Co-creation - You co-create your reality with the limit-less creative energies of All That Is.

Consciousness Unit - The theorized building blocks of realities. Elements of awarized energy that are telepathic and holographic.

Courage - Courage and Loving Understanding replace denial and intellectualization in the creation of Positive Realities.

Denial - The ego/intellect prevents the learning of Lessons by denying the truth of the matter.

Dimensions - Points of reference from one reality to the other with different vibrational wavelengths of consciousness.

Divine Day - The student attempts to live a complete waking day while maintaining contact with the Energy Personality.

Divine Will – The will is potentiated through ongoing contact and communication with Beings of Light. Also called Intent.

Ego/Intellect - The aspect of the personality that attempts to maintain the status quo reality.

Ecstasy - The positive emotion experienced in contact with the Divine.

Embodiment - Precepts are lived in the creation of improved realities.

Energy Personality – A being capable of transferring their thought energy inter-dimensionally to physical beings and sometimes using the physical abilities of those beings for communication.

Entity - Being not presently manifested on the physical plane. Also known as a Spirit.

Fourth-Dimensional Shift - Consciousness expands as the individual experiences an awareness of all Simultaneous Existences. Also called Unity of Consciousness Awareness.

Gestalts of Consciousness - Assemblages of Consciousness Units into Reality Constructs of all types.

gods - Consciousness personalized and projected outward into reality. A self-created projection of the developing ego.

Holographic Insert - Teaching aid of the nonphysical beings. Multisensory construct experienced with the Inner Senses.

Incarnation - To move oneself into another life experience on the physical plane.

Inner Sense - The Soul's perspective. Both the creator and the perceiver of Personal Realities.

Intellectualization - The aspect of the psyche that attempts to figure things out so that the status quo is maintained.

Intention - See Divine Will.

Lessons - Chosen life experiences of the Soul for further spiritual evolution.

Light Body - The etheric body of refined light.

Love - Love with a capital L is the force behind manifestation in the Third Dimension.

Moment Point - The current empowered moment of awakening. Exists as a portal to all points past, present and future and all Simultaneous Lives.

Mystery Civilizations - Foundational civilizations largely unknown to modern science. Some examples are Atlantis, Lemuria and GA.

Negative Emotion - Habitual creation of negative emotions creates enduring negative realities.

Negative Entities - Negative energies that roam the Universes in pursuit of their own power to dominate.

Personal Reality Field - The radius within your self-created world within which you have the most control in the creation of Reality Constructs.

Reality - That which one assumes to be true based on one's thoughts and experiences. Also called Perceived Reality.

Reality Creation - Consciousness creates reality.

Reincarnational Drama - Soul Family drama enacted to teach the participants a Lesson in Value Fulfillment.

Scientist of Consciousness - The researcher studies the phenomena within the Personal Reality Field by testing hypotheses in experimentation. See Precept.

Observer Perspective - Self-created aspect of consciousness that sees beyond the limitations of the ego/intellect. An intermediary position between the ego and the Soul Self.

Seth - An energy personality essence that has appeared within the mental environments of humans throughout the millennia to educate and inspire.

Simultaneous Lives - The multidimensional simultaneous experiences of Souls in incarnation.

Soul - The nonphysical counterpart to the physical human body, personality, and mentality. The spiritual aspect of the human.

Soul Evolution - The conscious learning of Lessons without denial or intellectualization.

Soul Family - The group of humans you incarnate with lifetime after lifetime to learn your Lessons together.

Spiritual Hierarchy - Beings of Light who have mastered multidimensional levels of experience throughout the Universes and have moved on to higher service in the evolution of all Souls.

The Christ - The embodiment of The Christ in your World. Also called World Teacher. First described in Seth Speaks.

The Council - Members of the Spiritual Hierarchy. Highly evolved beings that advise Souls on incarnations for their spiritual evolution.

The New World - The Positive Manifestation.

The Vanguard - Advocates for humanity and Mother Earth who incarnate together to lead progressive movements of various kinds.

Third Dimension - The physical plane of Earthly existence.

Trance State - The relaxed, focused state of awareness that allows the Scientist of Consciousness to conduct experiments and collect data.

Value Fulfillment - Consciousness seeks manifestation of itself into all realities via the fulfillment of all values.

Visionary - Reincarnated magicians, shamans, witches and healers in this current timeframe.

Percept - Perception creates reality in the Third Dimension through the Inner Senses..

Precept - Empowered concepts of manifestation. Example: you create your own reality.

I think we're going to have to do a book or two or three or four or many more to get the masses to see the problem ... Seth

MORE BOOKS?

Seth has promised to continue to communicate with us to further the awakening of humanity. This means that there will be an ongoing source of current, inspirational messages available from: **Seth Returns Publishing**

Communications from Seth on the Awakening of Humanity

9/11: The Unknown Reality of the World
The first original Seth book in two decades.
The Next Chapter in the Evolution of the Soul
The Scientist of Consciousness Workbook.
Thought Reality
Contains The Healing Regimen and Spiritual Prosperity.

The Trilogy

All That Is - Seth Comments on the Creative Source
Mystery Civilizations - Seth Answers Reader's Questions on Legendary Civilizations
Soul Mate/Soul Family - Lifetime After Lifetime We Learn Our Lessons Together

Seth - A Multidimensional Autobiography - in 2010

To order visit **sethreturns.com** or **amazon.com** Or ask your local metaphysical bookstore to carry the new Seth books.

CPSIA information can be obtained at www.ICGtesting.com
Printed in the USA
LVOW081955220312

274298LV00001B/54/P